D1495727

IT'S COOL TO LEARN ABOUT COUNTRIES

Social Studies Explorer

ETHIOPIA

➤ by Barbara A. Somervill

CHERRY LAKE PUBLISHING • ANN ARBOR, MICHIGAN

CHERRY
LAKE
Publishing

Published in the United States of America
by Cherry Lake Publishing
Ann Arbor, Michigan
www.cherrylakepublishing.com

Content Adviser: Getahun Benti, PhD, Professor, Department of History,
Southern Illinois University, Carbondale, Illinois

Book design: The Design Lab

Photo credits: Cover, ©Galyna Andrushko/Shutterstock, Inc. and ©iStockphoto.com/
marlenka; pages 4, and 29, ©Images of Africa Photobank/Alamy; page 5, ©GM Photo
Images/Alamy; pages 7 and 30, ©trevor kittelty/Shutterstock, Inc.; pages 9, 11 and
14, ©Matej Hudovernik/Shutterstock, Inc.; page 10, ©Suzanne Long/Alamy; page 12,
©Armin Baumgartner/Shutterstock, Inc.; page 13, ©Papilio/Alamy; pages 15 and 16,
©iStockphoto.com/Lingbeek; page 18, ©Benson HE/Shutterstock, Inc.; page 19, ©Lonely
Planet Images/Alamy; page 20, ©pdesign/Shutterstock, Inc.; page 21, ©vario images
GmbH & Co.KG/Alamy; pages 22 and 45, ©Clive Chilvers/Dreamstime.com; pages 24, 25
and 26, ©iStockphotos.com/jcarillet; pages 28, 33 and 38, ©Borderlands/Alamy; page 31,
©Peter Adams Photography Ltd/Alamy; page 34, ©INTERFOTO/Alamy; page 35, ©Gabriel
Openshaw/Alamy; page 37, ©Eye Ubiquitous/Alamy; page 40, ©dbimages/Alamy; page 41,
©Eva Gründemann/Dreamstime.com; page 43, ©Hemis/Alamy

Library of Congress Cataloging-in-Publication Data
Somervill, Barbara A.
  It's cool to learn about countries. Ethiopia/by Barbara A. Somervill.
      p. cm.—(Social studies explorer)
  Includes bibliographical references and index.
  ISBN-13: 978-1-61080-099-0 (library binding)
  ISBN-10: 1-61080-099-0 (library binding)
  1. Ethiopia—Juvenile literature. I. Title. II. Title: Ethiopia.
  DT373.S66 2012
  963—dc22   2010053943

Cherry Lake Publishing would like to acknowledge the work of The Partnership for
21st Century Skills. Please visit www.21stcenturyskills.org for more information.

Printed in the United States of America
Corporate Graphics Inc.
July 2011
CLFA09

TABLE OF CONTENTS

CHAPTER ONE

WELCOME TO ETHIOPIA!

●● Addis Ababa is the largest city in Ethiopia.

Selam! Welcome to Addis Ababa, Ethiopia's capital city. The first stop on our tour is the St. George Church Museum. Here you can see many important historic treasures. View helmets made from lions' manes, sharp curved swords, and the battle armor of Ethiopia's

ancient armies. After that, walk through the Mercato, one of the largest outdoor markets in Africa. It's crowded, noisy, and fascinating. Listen to shoppers bargain over everything from a few ounces of cinnamon to a couch.

Ethiopia is a diverse country, home to about 80 different ethnic groups. There's a lot to learn about Ethiopia, so let's get started.

➥ All sorts of goods can be found in the stalls of the Mercato.

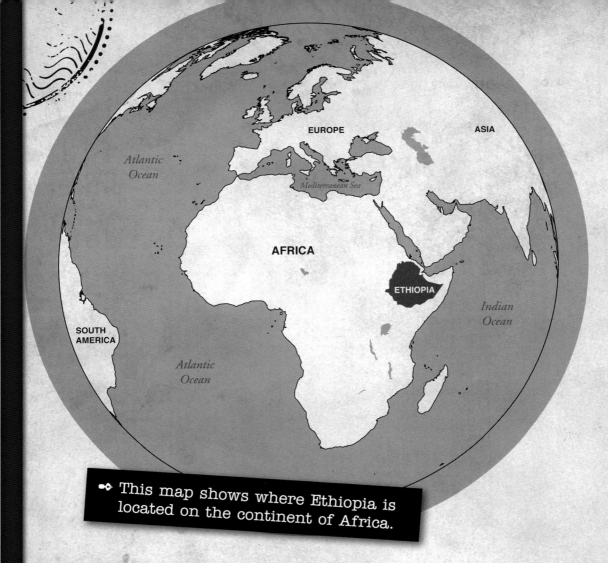

This map shows where Ethiopia is located on the continent of Africa.

Ethiopia is a large country in northeastern Africa. The country's total area is 435,184 square miles (1,127,121 square kilometers). That's the size of California and Texas put together. Addis Ababa is Ethiopia's largest city. With about 3 million people, it is about 10 times larger than any other city in the country. Smaller Ethiopian cities include Dire Dawa, Adama, Bahir Dar, Gonder, Mekele, and Jimma.

Many rivers cut through Ethiopia. The largest include the Abay (often called the Blue Nile), the Omo, the Awash, and the Wabe Shebele. Ethiopia is nicknamed the water tower because its many rivers run down from the country's highlands into neighboring countries. Ethiopia is landlocked, meaning that the country has no ocean ports. It must rely on shipping goods through its eastern neighbors, Somalia and Djibouti.

➥ The Blue Nile Falls are a popular tourist attraction.

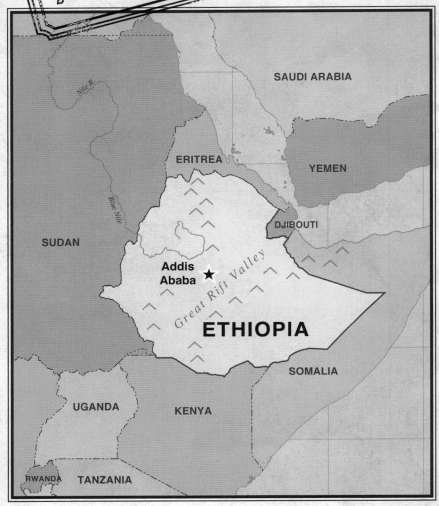

Place a piece of tracing paper over the map of Ethiopia and trace the country's borders. Mark the countries that border Ethiopia: Somalia, Djibouti, Eritrea, Sudan, and Kenya. Trace the path of the Blue Nile River and label it. Also label the Great Rift Valley, which runs through Ethiopia. Place a star for Addis Ababa, marking it as the capital city. Then use an atlas to look up and add additional details to your map.

Nearly half of Ethiopia is on the Ethiopian **Plateau**. It is mountainous land, covered with farms. The Great Rift Valley cuts through the plateau. To the east of the valley are the high peaks of the Eastern Highlands. From there the land gently slopes down to lowland plains. The eastern land is dry and suffers from long-term **droughts**. West of the Great Rift Valley, the highlands rise up toward the Simien Mountains, the highest peaks in Ethiopia. Many mountains in the Simien range rise more than 13,000 feet (4,000 meters). The country's highest mountain is Ras Dejen at 15,158 feet (4,620 m).

◆◆ Part of the Simien Mountain range is set aside as a national park.

The Great Rift Valley is a crack in the land that runs through Ethiopia from the northeast to the south. It is a region of volcanoes, earthquakes, deep valleys, and salty lakes. Parts of the Great Rift Valley are lush with plant life. Other areas are bare **salt flats**.

Ethiopia lies just north of the **equator**. Some people might expect that the climate always would be hot and steamy, like many other countries along the equator. Ethiopia is among the hottest countries on Earth. Ethiopia's climate, however, varies from region to region. High up in the mountain regions, the temperatures are usually cooler.

The Danakil Desert lies in the Great Rift Valley. It is a bleak land filled with salt deposits. It is also one of the hottest places on Earth. Temperatures in the Danakil Desert regularly rise above 120 degrees Fahrenheit (49 degrees Celsius).

Ethiopia enjoys two distinct seasons, wet and dry. The wet season comes at two different times. The country has a period of light rains from late February to the end of April. Heavy rains fall from June to September. The rest of the year is dry. Unfortunately, there are years when the rains fail to come. Then long periods of drought grip Ethiopia, destroying crops and killing cattle.

Ethiopia has an interesting variety of animals and plants. More than 275 species of mammals live in the country. At the Simien Mountains National Park, visitors can see gelada baboons plucking grasses and herbs for

⇢ Baboons are one of the only kinds of monkeys that live in dry environments.

their morning meal. The baboons chatter to each other and scurry about. Elsewhere in the park, a Walia ibex, a relative of the goat, scrambles over sharp rocks on a narrow cliffside path. Ethiopia is also home to 860 species of birds. The largest include bearded vultures, which have impressive 10-foot (3 m) wingspans. Snakes and lizards are common, and 324 types of butterflies flutter among the thousands of plants native to the country.

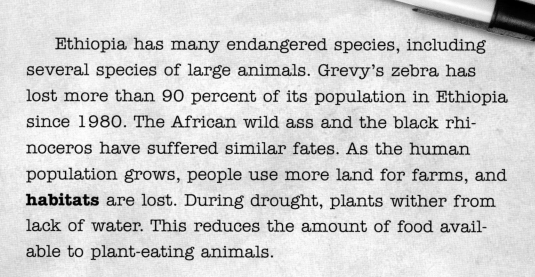

The Ethiopian wolf, also called the Simien fox and the red jackal, is native to the highlands. The wolves live in the Bale and Simien mountain ranges above 10,000 feet (3,000 m). Ethiopian wolves feed on giant mole rats, grass rats, and hares. They are the rarest **canid** in the world. Fewer than 500 remain worldwide.

Ethiopia has many endangered species, including several species of large animals. Grevy's zebra has lost more than 90 percent of its population in Ethiopia since 1980. The African wild ass and the black rhinoceros have suffered similar fates. As the human population grows, people use more land for farms, and **habitats** are lost. During drought, plants wither from lack of water. This reduces the amount of food available to plant-eating animals.

Ethiopia's national parks and preserves are helping to save endangered species. Once, only about 50 Walia ibex survived. Now, there are about 500 of these animals. Ethiopia's government is working to preserve its land and the animals that live there. Today, populations of Ethiopian wolves and gelada baboons are growing.

❖ Gelada baboons are not true baboons, but they are closely related.

AT WORK IN ETHIOPIA

➡ Planting seeds by hand is very hard work.

In a field fed by a local stream, a farmer bends to plant **teff** seeds in the soil. He hopes that the rains will come this year and that the teff will thrive. If it rains, he will be able to feed his family. If it rains, he will have grain to sell at the market. That is the constant worry for Ethiopian farmers: Will it rain? In recent years, the rain has often failed to come.

Some Ethiopian farmers raise several kinds of livestock.

Ethiopia's economy depends on agriculture. Farming represents 80 percent of the country's **exports** and 85 percent of its jobs. The largest agricultural employer is the coffee industry. More than 12 million people depend on coffee for their jobs. Farmers also grow wheat and teff, fruits, vegetables, and herbs. They raise cattle and chickens. Shepherds tend flocks of sheep, and goatherds raise goats. In Ethiopia, lambs and goats are sometimes eaten for dinner, if people can afford them. But when it does not rain, livestock cannot be fed and watered, crops fail, and people go hungry.

IMPORT EXPORT

The value of Ethiopia's **imports** is more than 4 times the value of the exports. Ethiopia imports food products, oil products, chemicals, machinery, cars and trucks, cereal grains, and fabrics. The country exports coffee, animal hides and skins, gold, leather, and oilseeds. Who do they trade with? See the chart below.

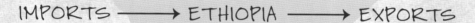

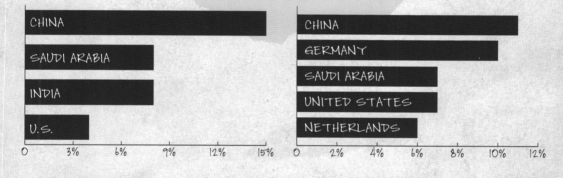

IMPORTS ⟶ ETHIOPIA ⟶ EXPORTS

IMPORTS		EXPORTS	
CHINA	(~15%)	CHINA	(~11%)
SAUDI ARABIA	(~8%)	GERMANY	(~10%)
INDIA	(~8%)	SAUDI ARABIA	(~7%)
U.S.	(~3.5%)	UNITED STATES	(~6.5%)
		NETHERLANDS	(~6%)

Imports scale: 0, 3%, 6%, 9%, 12%, 15%
Exports scale: 0, 2%, 4%, 6%, 8%, 10%, 12%

Nearly 40 percent of Ethiopia's people live in poverty. The average income per year equals about $108. There is little industry, although the country does produce **textiles**, chemicals, metals, and cement. When agriculture fails, there are few industry jobs for farmers who leave the land. Mining is limited to small amounts of gold, platinum, iron, and salt. The lack of industry means that Ethiopia must import most manufactured goods. About 6 million Ethiopians depend on free food from foreign countries for survival. During severe droughts, this number can increase to 8 million or more, about 1 in 10 Ethiopians.

The basic **currency** of Ethiopia is the birr. One birr can be divided into 100 santimi. In 2011 one U.S. dollar equaled a little less than 17 birr.

> ➥ The Amhara make up about one-fourth of Ethiopia's population.

Ethiopia adopted a **constitution** in 1995 that established a government with two houses of **parliament**. The House of the Federation has 112 members who represent the 69 nations, nationalities, and native peoples of Ethiopia. Each ethnic or native group has at least one representative. The representatives are chosen by regional councils. The number of representatives for each ethnic group depends on the population of that group. The Oromo is the largest ethnic group, but the

Afar, Amhara, Gamo, Gedeo, Hadiya, Somali, and Tigray all have several representatives. The Amhara is the second-largest ethnic group in Ethiopia.

The second house in Ethiopia's parliament is the House of the People's Representatives. It may have as many as 550 representatives. Ethiopia's citizens vote for these members. Members of both houses serve 5-year terms.

The Ethiopian flag features three horizontal stripes. The green stripe stands for fertile land. The yellow stripe represents justice and equality. The red stripe honors those who lost their lives to protect Ethiopia. The center of the flag is a blue circle with a yellow star and yellow rays shooting out from the star.

↦ Meles Zenawi has been the prime minister of Ethiopia since 1995.

Ethiopia's president and prime minister lead the country. The president is elected by a two-thirds majority of both houses of the parliament. The president is in charge of parliament meetings. The prime minister is the political leader of the country and holds office for 5 years. The prime minister is the leader of the political party that wins the most seats in the House of People's Representatives.

CHAPTER THREE

THE PEOPLE OF ETHIOPIA

➥ Ethiopia has a large population of children.

By population, Ethiopia is the 14th-largest country in the world and the second-largest in Africa. It is home to about 88 million people. Nearly half of the people are children below the age of 15.

Ethiopians belong to many different ethnic groups. About 30 million people belong to the Oromo ethnic group. The Oromo are divided into smaller subgroups and speak one of four versions of the Oromo language. The Oromo live in south-central and west-central Ethiopia. About 20 million people are Amhara. They live mainly in northwestern Ethiopia. The next largest ethnic groups are the Tigray and the Somali, which each have about 5 million people.

In 1974, the nearly complete skeleton of an ancient human being was found near Hadar, Ethiopia. The people who found the remains called her Lucy. Lucy was about 3 feet 8 inches (1.1 m) tall and lived sometime between 4 million and 2.7 million years ago.

➥ Some Ethiopian people dress in the traditional clothing of their ancestors.

More than four out of five Ethiopians live in rural areas, away from cities. When farming fails, Ethiopians seek work in cities. Ethiopia's cities grow every year.

The people of Ethiopia speak more than 70 different languages. About 30 percent of Ethiopians speak Amharic, which is the official language. In the southern regions, Oromigna, the language of the Oromo, is common. Many Ethiopians from the north speak Tigrinya or Tigray. In schools, children also learn English and Chinese.

AMHARIC

Here are key phrases in Amharic, the official language of Ethiopia, which might help a tourist traveling there.

Hello	Selam [seh-LAHM]
Good-bye to a man	Dahina hun [deh-hih-NAH hoon]
Good-bye to a woman	Dahina huqni [deh-hih-NAH hooq-nih]
Yes	Awo [AH-woh]
No	Aye [AH-ee]
Thank you	Ameseginalehu [AH-mah-say-quh-NAH-loh]
Excuse me	Yikerta [yayh-KEHR-tah]

❖ **People communicate with many different languages in Ethiopia.**

Traditionally, Ethiopians have followed clearly defined roles in families. Men worked and dealt with people outside the family. Women worked inside the home, cooked, cleaned, did the laundry, and raised the children. That situation is changing as Ethiopians move to cities. More women are getting jobs. More men are learning to help in the home.

➡ Ethiopian families enjoy spending time together.

ACTIVITY

GEBETA

A favorite activity of Ethiopian men is the ancient game of gebeta. It is played with beads, seeds, or pebbles. Two players place a long board between them. On the board are usually three rows with six holes in each row. The rules for playing gebeta change according to what part of the country the players live in. In one version of gebeta, the players begin with four beads in each hole, 72 beads in all. Each player "owns" the holes on their side of the board, plus three holes in the center row. Players take turns moving the beads and capturing their opponent's beads. A player wins by capturing the most beads.

Ethiopian students attend 6 years of elementary school. This is followed by 2 years of junior secondary school and 4 years of secondary school. Class sizes are large, and teachers may have as many as 65 students in one class. Many schools do not have enough books, paper, or pens for each student. The first 10 years of school are officially free, but some schools demand fees to help pay for books or supplies. Parents also have to buy school uniforms, which are required for all students.

➥ Ethiopian teachers work hard to make do with limited resources.

••➤ Many Ethiopian children learn to do chores at an early age.

Some families do not see any reason to send their children to school. They believe that boys should work on family farms. Girls should help their mothers with cooking, laundry, or taking care of younger children. More than 7 out of 10 Ethiopian children do not go to school. That situation is slowly changing.

CHAPTER FOUR

CELEBRATIONS

➻ Ethiopian churches are often beautiful, detailed buildings.

Religion is important in Ethiopian life. Many national holidays are holy days. Nearly 44 percent of Ethiopians belong to the Orthodox Christian Church. About 40 percent of people are Muslim, and about 10 percent are Protestant. The remaining 6 percent practice other religions. Most Amhara are Christian, while the Oromo mainly follow Islam. Smaller ethnic groups follow ethnic tribal beliefs.

Members of the Orthodox religion celebrate Christmas, Easter, saints' days, and other special events on the church calendar. They often **fast**, which means they cannot eat meat, eggs, or dairy products on certain days. In all, there are about 250 fast days for Ethiopian Orthodox Christians. This includes every Wednesday and Friday, as well as 56 days during Lent and 40 days before the Christmas season.

Ethiopian Christians participate in many religious celebrations throughout the year.

HOLIDAYS

January 7	Ethiopian Christmas
January 19	Timket (Feast of the Epiphany)
February 19	Martyr's Day
March 2	Victory of Adwa
March or April	Good Friday
May 1	Labor Day
September 11	New Year
September 27	Meskel (Feast of the True Cross)
Date varies	'Id al-Fitr (end of Ramadan)
Date varies	'Id al-Adha

Here are some of the national holidays celebrated in Ethiopia.

Ethiopians celebrate Christmas on January 7. On January 19 they celebrate the Feast of the Epiphany, called Timket. On Timket, people meet by a river, and priests bless the water and splash it on church members. The Feast of the True Cross, called Meskel, is held September 27. That festival celebrates the finding of what is believed to be the cross on which Jesus died. Ethiopians light large bonfires as part of this celebration.

Ethiopian children do not have much free time, but holidays are a time for play. Children like to play *Kukulu*. Gather some friends and try this game, which is a lot like hide-and-seek. The home base is called Mariam. Six or more children play, and one person is chosen to be the seeker. That person stands on Mariam and shouts "Kukulu!" The other children scatter and hide. The seeker has to find the hidden children. The hiders try to run back to Mariam before the seeker catches them. Winners are those who do not get caught.

➥ Kukulu can be played just about anywhere.

Ethiopia's Muslims follow the teachings of the Prophet Muhammad. Islamic teaching encourages Muslims to pray five times a day and read the Qur'an, the Muslim holy book. The holiest time for Muslims is Ramadan, a monthlong period of fasting. 'Id al-Fitr, a great feast that ends Ramadan, features much music and family fun.

Muhammad

Ethiopia follows its own calendar, which is different from the Gregorian calendar used in most of the rest of the world. The Ethiopian calendar has 12 months of 30 days and a 13th month of 5 days. On leap year, the 13th month has a 6th day.

→ Many Ethiopians have large families.

Family is central to life in Ethiopia. A child's name is important, and many Ethiopians hold naming ceremonies for newborns. Traditionally, parents chose husbands and wives for their children, and the bride and groom did not meet until the wedding. This still happens, but now some Ethiopians do not allow their parents to arrange their marriages.

Funerals bring friends and relatives together. They bear the responsibility for burying the dead. An Orthodox funeral includes chanting and readings in Ge'ez, an ancient language of Ethiopia. Everyone mourns together and goes to the burial together. For an important person in the community, a funeral may have hundreds or even thousands of mourners.

Ethiopians do not start their days at midnight like people in Western countries do. The day begins at the time we call 7 a.m. Ethiopians call this one o'clock.

CHAPTER FIVE

WHAT'S FOR DINNER?

➻ Spices and grains are just a few of the many ingredients available at Ethiopian markets.

Early in the day, the people of Addis Ababa head to the open-air market to shop. Heavy sacks of teff will be bought and turned into *injera*, a thin platter-size bread served in some parts of Ethiopia. Merchants line up to sell beef, chicken, lamb, and goat. Baskets of lemons and limes, bananas, grapes, figs, and pomegranates fill stall tables with their sweet scents. Hot red peppers, herbs, and other spices are sold by the ounce. Lab—a soft, lemony cheese—is sold in slabs, wrapped in banana leaves.

At home the family gathers around a small, flat, woven table after the food has been prepared. A basin and warm water are brought in, and everyone washes their hands. The cook lays injera or some other kind of bread on a large platter, which is placed on the table.

➥ Ethiopians eat meals with their families.

Ethiopians do not use knives, forks, or spoons. They tear off a piece of bread and use it to scoop up stew or cheese. Most Ethiopians eat only with their right hands, though left-handed people eat with their left hands. Ethiopians do not have dessert, but kitfo, a dish of raw ground beef, is thought of as a special treat to finish a dinner.

She spoons helpings of stews, vegetables, and salads onto the bread. Then it's time to eat.

Dinner is frequently *wat*, a spicy stew that is the national dish of Ethiopia. Wat can be made with beef, chicken, lamb, or goat. Mixed with *berbere*, a spicy paste, wat may be so hot that it burns the top of your mouth. The berbere spice mixture is a blend of ginger, cardamom, coriander, cloves, nutmeg, cinnamon, garlic, oil, and plenty of pepper.

➼ Injera is cooked on a large, flat pan made of clay. The pan is placed on three stones.

The Oromo eat large amounts of dairy products—milk, butter, and cheese. They enjoy *anan ititu*, a drink that is like thick milk. Breakfast is usually *marqa*—which is made from wheat, butter, and boiling water—or *qinche*, another cereal dish.

Muslims and Orthodox Christians do not eat pork. Orthodox Christians cannot eat meat, milk, cheese, or butter when they fast. Instead they eat stews made from legumes such as lentils, chickpeas, peanuts, and field peas. The legumes are cooked, mixed with berbere, and ground into a powder. The powder, called *mitin shiro*, can be cooked with oil and eaten cold with bread. It can also be added to stews for flavor. Some vegetarians may also eat *alicha*, a stew of peas, onions, and spices. It is similar to wat but is cooked without berbere.

Alicha is a tasty and filling dish.

Ethiopians believe that their homeland is the birthplace of coffee. Tradition claims that a goatherd herding his goats came upon a shrub with berries. He roasted the berries and brewed up the first pot of coffee.

The highlight of every Ethiopian dinner is coffee. Fresh coffee beans are washed, brought to the table, and roasted over small tabletop stoves. The beans crackle and pop in the roasting pan, filling the air with a rich coffee scent. The host puts roasted beans in a wooden bowl and crushes them into powder. The coffee grounds and water are brought to a boil in a pot. Then guests are served an absolutely fresh cup of coffee.

So sit down with friends, relax, and enjoy a delicious meal of stews and bread. It is the perfect way to begin to explore Ethiopia.

◆ Coffee shops are popular in large cities such as Addis Ababa.

Vegetable stews are common in Ethiopia. Atkilt alicha is a delicious and healthy cabbage dish. Have an adult help you with the chopping and cooking.

Atkilt Alicha

INGREDIENTS
½ cup (125 milliliters) olive oil
4 carrots, sliced
1 onion, sliced
1 teaspoon (5 ml) salt
½ teaspoon (2 ml) black pepper
½ teaspoon (2 ml) cumin
¼ teaspoon (1 ml) turmeric
½ head cabbage, shredded
5 potatoes, peeled and cut into cubes

INSTRUCTIONS

1. Heat the olive oil in a skillet over medium heat.
2. Cook the carrots and onion in the oil for about 5 minutes.
3. Stir in the salt, pepper, cumin, turmeric, and cabbage and cook for another 15 to 20 minutes.
4. Add the potatoes and cover the pan. Reduce the heat to medium-low and cook for 20 to 30 minutes, or until the potatoes are soft.

Serve with injera or another flat bread. Enjoy!

● Pick up your vegetables at the market and enjoy some delicious Ethiopian cuisine!

canid (CAY-nid) a member of the wolf or dog family

constitution (kon-stih-TOO-shuhn) a document that sets up a government system

currency (KUR-unt-see) paper money or coins

droughts (DROUTS) periods of little or no rain

equator (ee-KWAY-tuhr) an imaginary line halfway between Earth's north and south poles

exports (EK-sportss) goods shipped to another country to be sold

fast (FAST) to go without eating food or certain types of food during a set period

habitats (HA-buh-tats) places where plants or animals naturally live

imports (IM-ports) goods one country buys from another country

parliament (PAHR-luh-muhnt) the lawmaking body of a country

plateau (plah-TOH) flat, raised land

salt flats (SAWLT FLATS) a flat area of land encrusted with salt, formed by evaporation of a body of water

teff (TEF) a type of grain native to Ethiopia

textiles (TEK-stylz) cloths or goods produced by weaving or knitting

FOR MORE INFORMATION

ETHIOPIA

Books

Heinrichs, Ann. *Ethiopia*. New York: Children's Press, 2005.

Pohl, Kathleen. *Looking at Ethiopia*. New York: Gareth Stevens, 2009.

Thimmesh, Catherine. *Lucy Long Ago: Uncovering the Mystery of Where We Came From*. Boston: Houghton Mifflin Harcourt, 2009.

Web Sites

Embassy of Ethiopia
www.ethiopianembassy.org/
At this Web site, you can learn about Ethiopian people and culture.

Ethiopianow
www.ethiopianow.com/music/
What do Ethiopians listen to on the radio? Connect to this Web site, and you will find out!

Lonely Planet—Ethiopia
www.lonelyplanet.com/ethiopia
Check out this guide that helps you decide what to see and do in Ethiopia.

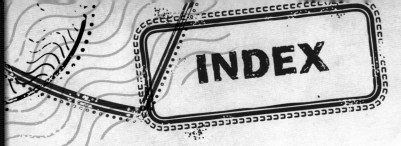

ABOUT THE AUTHOR

Barbara Somervill has never been to Africa, but she has read a lot about the countries, their cultures, and their folktales. Ethiopia is on her wish list for vacations. One of Somervill's favorite recent experiences was dining with friends at an Ethiopian restaurant in Washington, DC. It was a rare treat, breaking injera with friends.